1100L

by Megan Howard

Lerner Publications Company
Minneapolis

For Ashleigh and Emily

Copyright © 1999 Lerner Publications Company and Megan Howard

Lerner Publications Company
241 First Avenue North
Minneapolis, MN 55401

Website address: www.lernerbooks.com

Library of Congress Cataloging-in-Publication Data

Howard, Megan
    Christopher Reeve / Megan Howard.
      p.   cm. — (A & E biography)
    Includes bibliographical references and index.
    Summary: A biography of the actor who became well known for his movie portrayal of Superman and for his activities in support of nerve damage research since the riding accident that left him a quadriplegic.
    ISBN 0-8225-4945-X (alk. paper)
    1. Reeve, Christopher, 1952– —Juvenile literature. 2. Actors— United States—Biography—Juvenile literature. 3. Quadriplegics— United States—Biography—Juvenile literature. [1. Reeve, Christopher, 1952– . 2. Actors. 3. Quadriplegics. 4. Physically handicapped.] I. Title. II. Series.
PN2287.R292H68 1999
791.43'028'092—dc21
[B]   98-8200

Manufactured in the United States of America
1 2 3 4 5 6 – JR – 04 03 02 01 00 99

CONTENTS

Christopher Reeve gets advice from a member of the U.S. equestrian team before participating in a celebrity event in Gladstone, New Jersey, in June 1994.

Introduction

A flurry of activity swarmed about Commonwealth Park in Culpeper, Virginia. Equestrians, horses, coaches, and spectators awaited the second event in the Commonwealth Dressage and Combined Training Association's horse trials that Memorial Day weekend in 1995. Eagerly walking the course on Saturday afternoon, Christopher Reeve carefully noted the peculiarities of the ground and each of the jumps to determine the safest and fastest route over them. He had already examined them the day before, but like all good riders, he never took chances. Knowing what to expect would help Reeve guide his horse through the 15-obstacle course and gain an advantage over the 300 other competitors.

Judges awarded and deducted points for the three different categories—dressage, cross-country jumping, and stadium jumping—in this and similar events. In dressage, riders are awarded points for completing several required technical elements well and showing that their horses are calm and obedient. Cross-country jumping demonstrates the horse's boldness and ability to clear big hurdles. Stadium jumping combines the qualities of both dressage and cross-country jumping.

Reeve, who likes competition, was thrilled to be moving up from the "novice" category—the first level of competition—to "training." He knew he was ready for the challenge of the higher level, where there were more and higher obstacles.

Earlier that day, May 27, Reeve had competed in the dressage phase of the trials and placed in the middle of the finishers, a respectable showing considering it was his first attempt at the new level. Saturday's event, cross-country jumping, would be the most difficult part of the competition.

When he was satisfied that he knew the course, Reeve finished putting on his riding clothes. Then he went to the stables to get his horse, a roan gelding named Eastern Express but called Buck. He swung his

Reeve jumps during a cross-country event in Southampton, Massachusetts, on May 14, 1995.

long leg over his mount's back, and together they took off for the warm-up area.

Earlier that day Reeve had told a reporter, "Horse jumping is the most dangerous thing I do." But today there was no need for concern. He had trained for eight years, competed regularly, and wore his protective gear. He hadn't fallen off a horse in over a year. In fact, Reeve was impressed by how quickly he and his new horse had learned to work together. "[Buck had] been jumping beautifully, beautifully. We were a wonderful team," he said later.

After warm-up, Reeve was ready to take his turn in the competition. He guided his horse, easily clearing the first two jumps, and prepared to leap over the third one, a stack of timbers just over three feet high. It was an easy jump, rating a three on a ten-point scale. Leaning forward, Reeve headed for the obstacle at about 500 yards per minute.

Suddenly, Buck stopped, refusing to clear the hurdle. Horses take their orders from their riders. Jumping horses learn what to do by observing the rider's body signals. Reeve had failed to clearly tell the horse what to do as they approached the jump. "You know, you really need a strong leg at that point," the actor later explained. With Buck's bridle tangled in his hands, Reeve flew over the animal's head and cleared the jump by himself. Unable to free his hands to break the fall, he hit the ground headfirst and gasped "I can't breathe."

As Buck galloped back to the barn, an anesthesiologist watching the competition rushed over and performed mouth-to-mouth resuscitation on Reeve. While one of the judges called for an ambulance, the doctor kept Reeve alive by breathing for him until the paramedics arrived in an ambulance about a minute later. It was clear to everyone who had seen the accident that Reeve had suffered a serious injury.

Because his spine was swelling, every moment was crucial. But the paramedics couldn't be careless in their rush to save Reeve since the wrong move could cause further damage to his fragile condition. The paramedics worked quickly and carefully to secure Reeve's body and prevent further movement. They placed him in the ambulance and rushed him to the emergency room (ER) at Culpeper Medical Center.

Bill Maloney, the doctor in charge of the emergency room, took over Reeve's care once he came through the hospital doors, strapped to a gurney. Maloney and his staff injected the patient with methylprednisolone, a synthetic steroid that reduces swelling in the spine. The Culpeper hospital couldn't provide any other lifesaving care for Reeve, however. They didn't have much expertise in spinal cord injury (SCI) treatment.

The University of Virginia Medical Center, a larger hospital about 50 miles away in Charlottesville, had better facilities and staff with a great deal of knowledge and experience in spinal cord injury. Every second mattered, so Dr. Maloney called for *Pegasus*, a helicopter equipped with medical supplies, to fly Reeve to Charlottesville.

His wife, Dana, who had stayed at the motel, got a call, telling her what had happened. She and their son, Will, rushed to the hospital. Will watched as hospital workers put his unconscious father in the helicopter. Unable to understand much of what was happening in front of him, the terrified little boy believed that his dad was going to die.

The doctors and nurses around Reeve thought so, too. The medical staff told Dana to say good-bye to her husband and to think about funeral arrangements. When the helicopter lifted into the air, nobody knew if he would survive the trip to Charlottesville.

Christopher Reeve during his senior year at Princeton Day School

Chapter **ONE**

WORLD PREMIERE

CHRISTOPHER REEVE MADE HIS FIRST SCENE-stealing entrance at Lenox Hill Hospital in New York City on September 25, 1952. His parents, Franklin and Barbara Reeve, didn't mind being upstaged by the birth of their first son.

The infant's mother and father brought Christopher home to the family's apartment at 535 East 88th Street. They had married over Thanksgiving break in 1951. Franklin was a student working on his doctoral degree at Columbia University in New York City. Barbara had attended Vassar and Barnard Colleges for a short time before and after the marriage, but she concentrated on caring for Chris after he was born.

The baby had some impressive ancestors. Both his

Barbara Johnson, Reeve's mother, at her home in Princeton, New Jersey

parents came from wealthy families. On his father's side, Reeve's great-grandfather, Colonel Richard d'Olier, was the president of Prudential Insurance Company beginning in 1938. His children and grandchildren went to exclusive schools and were reared with all the luxuries money could buy. But even though Franklin Reeve came from an extremely wealthy family, he had rejected their money and paid for his education at Columbia by loading and unloading boats on the docks across the Hudson River in Hoboken, New Jersey.

The next year, Christopher had a playmate. A baby brother named Benjamin was born on October 6,

1953, when Chris was just one year old. "My mother found herself married, with me and my younger brother, when she was 20," he later told an interviewer. In March 1955, the situation for Barbara got even more difficult when Franklin Reeve moved out of the apartment. The couple divorced in 1956.

The boys and their mother moved to Princeton, New Jersey, on December 31, 1956, because their apartment building was going to be torn down to put up a high-rise building. Barbara was already familiar with the area since several of her family members and her ex-husband had attended Princeton University. She decided her young sons would benefit from the good education the community's public schools provided and enrolled Chris at Nassau Street School, which was within walking distance of their home.

Caught up in their own anger, Barbara and Franklin made Chris feel as if he had to choose between them. "My mother and father were always fighting over me, and therefore canceled each other out," he has said about the years after the divorce. Because they both said negative things about the other, Chris didn't feel he could love one better than the other. Although he was just a child, he felt responsible for his parents' happiness. Because of that difficult duty, "I never had time to be a kid," he has said.

In June 1959, when Chris was six years old, his mother married Tristam Johnson, a wealthy stockbroker. Johnson already had four children of his own.

Chris and Ben continued to spend time with their father, sometimes going on sailing expeditions in the summer or skiing trips in the winter. Chris especially liked to take trips to the Pocono Lake Preserve, where his grandmother had a home. When they returned to Princeton, however, his father stopped in front of the next-door neighbor's house and made Chris and Ben walk from there. By the time Chris was eight, his parents stopped speaking to each other completely.

In the midst all of the family turmoil, Chris managed to find some joy, however. "Princeton absolutely formed me," he said. "It set me on a path that brought me great, great happiness." As young boys, Chris and Ben set up empty boxes on their front porch and pretended to be pirates sailing the seas. They both played on the same Little League baseball team, one catching while the other pitched. Their activities weren't always fun and games, however, because the boys often competed with each other.

The two brothers also participated in peewee hockey together. Chris was seven years old when he heard about the sports program and decided he'd like to try it. Because his mother didn't get the application form in on time, he learned that he'd have to wait until the next year to try out for the team. Instead of waiting another year, Chris woke up early in the morning and rode his bike to Baker Rink at Princeton University, where a game was in session. Between periods of the hockey game, Chris skated onto the ice so the peewee league organizer, John Bernard, could see how determined he was to be part of the program. Finally, Bernard agreed that Chris could join—but under one condition: he had to be goalie. Chris had hoped to make the goals, not dodge the puck, but since it was the only way he was going to participate, he agreed. He soon learned that goalie could be a star position, and he continued in that spot.

Chris also enjoyed music. His family were members of Princeton's Nassau Presbyterian Church, and he sang in the children's choir. When he was eight years old, Chris found something he was very good at—playing the piano. At that point in his life, it was the pastime he enjoyed most, and he dreamed of performing in front of an audience. "I always wanted to be a pianist right from when I was a kid," he explained.

Chris also loved books and filled his quiet moments reading Greek mythology. In the winter, when he wanted to be with his friends, he went over to the lake near his house and played ice hockey. One year when the lake thawed, Chris and Ben set their pet goldfish free.

Reeve and a costar sing during a school performance of Little Mary Sunshine.

Chapter **TWO**

SUPER BOY

AT THE BEGINNING OF FOURTH GRADE, BARBARA transferred Chris to Princeton Day School so he could have a greater academic challenge than his public school had provided. As he sat in science class that year, his mind wandered. He wasn't very interested in the subject, so he was relieved when a stranger walked through the door. The man explained that he was from the local arts group and asked if there were any students interested in singing in a performance of *The Yeoman of the Guard* at the McCarter Theatre in Princeton.

Chris immediately raised his hand, "mostly to get out of science class," he said. He did have a nice soprano singing voice, however, and after his audition, he was accepted for the part. Rehearsals and perfor-

Reeve, third from the right in the front row, *in* Finian's Rainbow

mances took him away from his schoolwork, but the
school's headmaster said that as long as Chris made
up all of his homework, he could be in the play.
"[B]eing somebody else took me away from a lot of
things I was not prepared to deal with," Reeve explained, referring to his difficult home life.

As Chris pursued his acting interest, big events were
happening at home. Chris's half-brother Jeffrey was
born in April 1961, and another half-brother, Kevin,
arrived two years later.

Chris tried to distinguish himself from his siblings.
He earned more and more small parts at the theater
and made many new friends there. He felt as though

he had been adopted by McCarter's company of actors and that the theater was more of a home than his parents' houses had ever been. "It was a place of great security and great growth," he said.

Reeve continued to sing, play the piano, participate in sports, and try new things. He was a star pupil, but soon he realized that he loved to act more than anything. In addition to productions at McCarter, he performed in school plays. To prepare for his part as a Scottish housemaid in Agatha Christie's play *Witness for the Prosecution,* Chris learned to speak with a

Reeve, standing third from the left, *in a 1968 production of* How to Succeed in Business without Really Trying *at the Williamstown Theatre Festival*

Scottish brogue. Because he could also sing, he could play the lead part in musicals as well as dramas.

When he was 14 years old, Reeve acted in *Finian's Rainbow,* which was directed by Milton Lyon at McCarter. "You should be careful about what you want and what you do," Lyon told the teenager, "because you may be the one in a million who makes it."

Chris didn't love the stage solely because he was a good actor. He also enjoyed the escape from reality. In addition to his unhappy home life, he also had physical problems that he wanted to forget. By the time he was 14, he was six feet two inches tall. Because he suffered from Osgood-Schlatter's disease, his tendons didn't

Enthusiastic theatergoers line up at the McCarter Theatre in Princeton, New Jersey.

Reeve, back row left, *was the tenor in the Princeton Day School Madrigal Singers.*

grow as fast as his bones. Fluid gathered in his joints, and he couldn't move very well. "As a result, I was very, very awkward," Reeve said. "And enormous. I used to stand with my legs locked all the time."

Other characteristics also made Reeve stand out among his peers. "I was not a lot of laughs," he explained. As a teenager, Reeve spent much of his time thinking about the threat of a third world war. Many girls his age were not interested in the topic. Reeve has said, "That whole dating game was painful."

In this photo of the Princeton Day School hockey team, Reeve is first on the right in the front row.

Luckily, a desire to act gave Reeve something else to focus on. He began to think of performing as a career rather than a hobby. "I've never gone through any self-searching to decide what I can do best," he said. "Acting is what I do best."

Reeve constantly sought ways to improve, however. The summer after ninth grade, he attended nearby Lawrenceville School to take acting workshops with professionals from New York City's theater community. During the summer of 1968, he attended Williamstown Theatre Festival's apprenticeship program. The apprentices took acting, voice, and movement classes. They also attended seminars conducted by the theater's professional actors and directors and presented scenes for the company to critique. In addition, every student received training in the various theater departments, such as lighting, props, and publicity. The experience fueled Chris's desire to be onstage.

Apprentices could audition for small roles in the theater's productions and act alongside professional actors. The eager teenager took advantage of the opportunity and appeared in four out of seven plays—*Iphigeneia at Aulis, Camino Real, Galileo,* and *How to Succeed in Business without Really Trying.*

When Chris was 16, his mother gave him a Steinway piano so he could continue to pursue his love of music. During the school year, he also served as assistant coordinator of the school orchestra, worked on the literary magazine, and sang in the madrigal choir. Somehow he still had enough time to become an ice hockey letterman for the school's varsity team.

By the time Chris graduated in June 1970, he had an agent to arrange professional auditions and an Actors' Equity card—membership in a union for actors that sets minimum salaries and provides them with benefits, such as insurance. Some theaters hire only union members, so any actors who wish to perform on those stages must join the union. That summer, at 17, Chris toured with the company of *Forty Carats.* The cast included Eleanor Parker, a three-time Oscar nominee.

The Cornell University library and clock tower in Ithaca, New York, where Reeve attended college

Chapter **THREE**

MAKING IT

CHRISTOPHER'S PARENTS ENCOURAGED HIS ACTING career but insisted that he attend college. He chose to enroll at Cornell University in Ithaca, New York, because as he has said, "It's snowed in from October to May." With snow covering the roads, it would be difficult to drive out of town to auditions, so he could concentrate on schoolwork.

He sang with the Sage Chapel Choir, competed on the sailing team, worked at radio station WVBR, and acted in Cornell productions of *The Good Woman of Szechuan, Waiting for Godot,* and *A Winter's Tale.*

Each year when the snow melted and the roads cleared, Reeve hopped in his 1970 Fiat and drove to New York City for tryouts. His agent set up auditions

Christopher Reeve, second from the left, *plays Dumaine in the Old Globe Theatre's production of* Love's Labour's Lost *for the 1972 Shakespeare Festival.*

around his class schedule each semester. Occasionally the two conflicted, and Chris chose to miss class rather than lose out on an exciting role. "Somehow I managed to balance the academic and professional sides of my life," he said. One way he managed the difficult juggling act was to wake up at 3:00 A.M. in order to make it to New York City in time for his auditions.

The effort paid off, however. Reeve took off the fall session of his junior year so he could perform at the Old Globe Theatre's Shakespeare Festival in San Diego, California, as part of the professional repertory company. A repertory theater performs different plays on alternating days, so the actors must learn parts for two or three different plays during a single season and might perform several plays in one week. Reeve appeared in *The Merry Wives of Windsor, Love's Labour's Lost,* and *King Richard III.*

During the spring and summer of his junior year, Reeve went to Europe to study more about repertory theaters. He flew into Glasgow, Scotland, then slowly made his way to London. He stopped at theaters along the way to talk to actors and attend rehearsals as part of some research he was doing for a paper.

Reeve gained some professional experience, too. He worked as a "dogsbody" at London's Old Victory Theatre, better known as "Old Vic." "I was a glorified

During the summer of his junior year in college, Reeve worked as a "dogsbody" at the Old Vic Theatre in London, England.

Actor and teacher John Houseman

errand boy," he explained. One of his main duties was getting coffee for the actors. However, when the company began rehearsing for *The Front Page,* a play about journalism, his responsibilities increased. He coached the actors on how to speak with an American accent. Reeve then headed for Paris, France, and worked with the Comedie Française, a theater founded by King Louis XIV in the 17th century.

In 1973, during his senior year at Cornell, Reeve took classes at The Juilliard School—a prestigious music and arts school in New York City. He studied drama "under the legendary and terrifying John Houseman," as he described his mentor. Houseman appeared as law school professor Kingsfield in *The Paper Chase* that year, a role for which he won the

Best Supporting Actor Oscar in 1974. Houseman was a masterful teacher. One day in class, Reeve performed a scene from Tennessee Williams's *Summer and Smoke*. Afterward, Houseman called him into the teacher's office for a private conference. "Mr. Reeve, it is terribly important that you become a serious classical actor," he said sternly, then added, "unless, of course, they offer you a [truck]load of money."

Juilliard provided Reeve with intense technical training—especially in the areas of singing and movement. He also met Robin Williams, who became his roommate and friend. Although he was unknown at the time, Williams became a famous comedian, starring in movies and in the popular television series *Mork and Mindy*. On June 3, 1974, Reeve earned a Bachelor of Arts, with honors, from Cornell's College of Arts and Sciences.

While at Juilliard, Reeve assumed he'd act in regional theater his entire life. Then his first major break came. In 1974, he auditioned for a CBS soap opera called *Love of Life* and got the part of Ben Harper, a rich mafia hit man married to two women. At first, he appeared in only one or two episodes each week, but people loved to hate his nasty character. Soon he was appearing on the program every day.

Reeve was so convincing in his role that he suffered a few bruises because of it. One day while he was dining in a restaurant in New Hampshire, a *Love of Life* viewer recognized him and approached his table, but

Actor Robin Williams

she didn't ask for an autograph. "How dare you treat your poor pregnant wife that way?" she shouted, hitting him on the head with her purse.

With his earnings from the soap opera, Reeve took up a new hobby. He signed up for his first flying lessons with an instructor named Robert Hall in 1975. He continued taking lessons at Teterboro Flight Academy in New Jersey, where he gained enough experience to get his pilot's license.

After he'd saved "a few thousand dollars," Reeve bought himself a small, used airplane, a Cherokee 140. He took off from Teterboro Airport and flew across the United States, making stops along the way and camping out under the wings at night. He then returned to New York City. "I loved flying," he later said. "Everything about it."

On February 3, 1976, when he was only 23 years old, Reeve made his Broadway theater debut, playing Nicky in *A Matter of Gravity*. The role cast him as the grandson of the main character, who was portrayed by the great Katharine Hepburn. The famous actress had distinguished herself in theater and film and had twice won the Best Actress Oscar. Hepburn proved to be a charming yet intimidating character. "People say I acted with Katharine Hepburn. I acted near Katharine Hepburn," Reeve joked, meaning that his inexperience couldn't compare to her skilled performances.

Reeve, standing left, *made his Broadway debut in* A Matter of Gravity *with Katharine Hepburn,* seated.

Although Hepburn and Reeve grew to have a close relationship during the play's six-month tour throughout the country and its short run at New York City's Broadhurst Theatre, they got off to a difficult start. At his audition, Reeve approached the legendary actress and said, "I bring you greetings of one of your classmates at Bryn Mawr, my grandmother, Beatrice Lamb." Hepburn responded, "Oh, Bea, I never could stand her."

Clearly, Hepburn did not dislike Beatrice Lamb's grandson. "She had the most impact on my intentions as an actor," Reeve has said about her. The most important lesson she taught him was to bring himself into the parts he played. As a youth, he had been so busy hiding behind his characters that he hadn't realized how important his real-life experiences could be to the parts he played.

"I can remember her in the wings just before I was supposed to go on," Reeve recalled. "I was 23, on Broadway, and scared to death—and she's leaning on a cane, smiling and telling me, 'Be fascinating now, be fascinating.' Fascinating? I was trying not to pass out!"

Reeve's Broadway debut played a significant role for another reason. By then, Reeve's father had married Helen Schmidinger, and they had three children of their own—Mark, Brock, and Alison. Reeve had bought his parents and stepparents tickets in the same row for the opening night of the play. For the first time in 15 years, his parents spoke to each other.

"They buried the hatchet," he said proudly.

After 150 performances, *A Matter of Gravity* closed on April 13, 1976. By June, Reeve's personal and professional triumphs had dwindled. After two years on *Love of Life*, his contract ran out. Without any other roles at the time, Reeve flew his Cherokee 140 to California, but this time he didn't fly back for several months. Instead, he sat on a Santa Monica, California, beach and thought about what he should do with his future.

"I was sponging off friends, sleeping on couches, turning into a vegetable, and then one day I said this isn't right," he later explained. In November, he piloted his plane back to New York City and began putting his acting career together again.

In 1977, Christopher Reeve landed the title role in Superman: The Movie.

Chapter **FOUR**

THE AUDITION

WHEN REEVE RETURNED TO HIS ROACH-INFESTED one-room apartment in New York City late in 1976, he got to work. He auditioned for and won a part in a submarine movie called *Gray Lady Down*. Soon after that, Reeve was back on the stage, playing a supporting role in a Circle Repertory Company production of *My Life*. He earned about $85 per week.

By now Reeve had nine agents, and one of them contacted Lynn Stalmaster, who was in charge of casting for *Superman: The Movie*. For 18 months, the movie's producers had been considering Hollywood's list of top actors, searching for someone to play the title character. Robert Redford, James Caan, and Clint Eastwood had turned down the role. The producers

In 1976, Christopher Reeve won a role in the submarine movie Gray Lady Down.

had rejected Steve McQueen, Charles Bronson, and Sylvester Stallone. They'd even considered Bruce Jenner, who had won the decathlon gold medal at the 1976 Summer Olympics.

Stalmaster had seen Reeve's work and agreed that he seemed perfect to play a superhero. He just had to convince the producers—and Christopher Reeve. "I was a bit of a snob," Reeve admitted. "I thought it was beneath me. After all, I was a classical actor," even though he'd spent two years on a TV soap opera. In fact, he agreed to meet with the director, Richard Donner, and one of the movie's producers, Ilya Salkind, only because the meeting was in a convenient location. That morning Reeve had auditioned for a commercial for Dreft laundry detergent, and he was headed to Grand Central train station. The Sherry Netherland Hotel, where Donner and Salkind wanted him to meet them, was on the way.

The three men talked in a hotel suite, but Reeve said that Donner and Salkind didn't tell him very much about *Superman*. "At one point, Donner gave me his pair of glasses and asked me to try them on," he remembered. When the director and producer glanced at each other, Reeve said, "I knew I'd passed some sort of preliminary hurdle." The men had been looking for someone who could act and who possessed the Superman and Clark Kent look. As part of his disguise, Clark Kent wore glasses.

Reeve was right. He received two phone calls, during which he was asked to go to England and take a screen test for *Superman*. At a screen test, a camera films an actor as he or she performs so the director and producers can get an idea of how comfortable the actor appears on film. Reeve still thought he was too good an actor to appear in an epic movie about a comic book character. But Reeve finally decided, "Why pass up a free trip to England?"

By the time he tested at Shepperton Studios on January 30, 1977, production had already begun on the movie. Even without a star, carpenters and artists were creating sets in the production studios. The moviemakers had cast many of the minor roles, in-

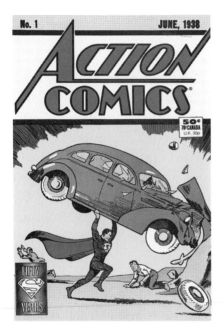

The Superman character is based on a comic book hero whose story was first published in 1938.

cluding Marlon Brando as Superman's father, Jor-El.

Reeve memorized dialogue and cues as if he already had the part—the same way he had prepared for all of his professional auditions. "I go in thoroughly prepared because that's a big step toward having confidence," he said.

The screen test required him to become two characters, Superman and Clark Kent—the superhero's everyday disguise. When Reeve showed up for the test, *Superman's* technical and creative team began to doubt themselves. The would-be superhero was sweating, and Superman was never supposed to seem troubled. Then Reeve stepped onto the balcony set and coolly fell into character, saying, "Good evening, Miss Lane."

Reeve confidently performed the two parts for the camera. Reeve said he could relax by taking the test with an "I-don't-care-if-I-get-it attitude." "I had the part, unofficially, by lunchtime," he explained to film critic Gene Siskel. But the Superman role would not officially be Reeve's until Warner Bros. executives viewed the screen test. Studios provide money and behind-the-scenes personnel for productions, and the executives wanted to be sure they had a star who would earn their money back for them.

Reeve also played Clark Kent, the mild-mannered newspaper reporter and Superman disguise. Margot Kidder played the reporter Lois Lane.

Finally, Donner phoned Reeve in mid-February 1977. When Reeve answered the phone, Donner told him, "Congratulations, you have been chosen to play the title role in our film, *Superman*." By that time, Reeve wanted the part. He had had a chance to read the entire script and liked it enough to commit to the movie.

Since publicity for the movie had begun three years earlier and the search for someone to play Superman had been going on for a year and a half, both Hollywood and the country were buzzing about the new, young actor who had finally been chosen. Photographers waited outside Reeve's apartment, hoping to snap a picture of the man who had become a movie sensation overnight.

Rushing to finalize the deal, Reeve's agents negotiated with the producers regarding the details of the actor's contract. Reeve received $250,000 and promised not to discuss the movie's plot until its release or to reveal any secrets about special effects. This was the first movie to attempt to realistically show a flying human being. If they could pull the feat off, the filmmakers would make movie history. Because the producers anticipated a blockbuster success, they also made Reeve commit to starring in the movie's sequel. He would receive some of the profits from the original movie and a larger portion from the sequel.

Even though he'd landed Hollywood's most talked-about role, Reeve still wasn't ready to play Superman. At six feet four inches, his 188-pound body was fine for the role of Clark Kent, but it would never convince the audience that he was Superman. Reeve began working with David Prowse, a bodybuilder who had worn the Darth Vader costume in *Star Wars*. Morning workouts included running and training outdoors. Then Reeve spent two hours lifting weights. After that, he rehearsed flying and landing for 90 minutes. The routine also included gulping down four high-protein meals every day.

At the end of the first day's workout, "I went into the locker room and heaved," Reeve said. With the role of a lifetime on the line, he stuck it out for 10 weeks. After so much training, Reeve was definitely ready to make the world believe a man—or at least a superman—could fly.

Reeve had to switch characters in the Superman movies, playing two different roles.

Chapter **FIVE**

ON LOCATION

To save money, Donner shot *Superman: The Movie* and parts of *Superman II* at the same time. Much of the first movie tells the story of how Superman came to Earth from the planet Krypton, gained his super-human powers, and then used them to fight the villain Lex Luthor.

All indoor scenes were filmed in London's Shepperton Studios, where Reeve had taken his screen test. Scenes that took place in the fictitious Metropolis, where Clark Kent worked for *The Daily Planet* and Superman fought crime, were shot in New York City. Other scenes were filmed in Spain and Australia. Scenes involving the Kents's hometown, Smallville, Kansas, were shot in that state.

Even after Donner knew where he was going to direct the movie, he wasn't sure exactly how he would do it. Initially the moviemakers had planned to suspend Reeve from wires that vibrated so much that they'd create a strobe effect on film, making them invisible. When that failed, they covered the wires with black felt, but that didn't work either.

Finally, the technical crew created a flying mechanism with wires, a pole, and some plaster casts. In the studio, the crew built tracks in the ceiling so wires that were the same color as the background could slide back and forth and from side-to-side. This device allowed Reeve to sail and swoop through the air with ease. The crew couldn't hide the wires from the camera

Reeve, right, *talks on the movie set with director Richard Donner.*

Getting Superman to fly created many challenges for the movie's technical crew.

for close-ups, however. For those shots, they attached a horizontal pole along Reeve's spine. Long, fast shots were accomplished by shooting plaster casts—painted to look like Superman—out of a cannon.

Once the technical problems were solved, it was up to Reeve to convince the moviegoers that he was as comfortable in the air as the comic book Superman. The actor went straight to the source to observe how the caped crusader took off, flew, and landed on the page. Still, it was easier to draw a character doing these things than to show a live person actually doing them. Reeve's early years in a hockey rink came in handy, but that experience didn't solve all his problems. "Superman usually came in sideways the way a hockey player stops," he said. "But if you land from 75 yards in the air, it takes some practice. You come in at about the same speed as a parachute jumper."

The costumers also played an important role in creating the illusion of flight. Reeve wore six different capes. Wires were sewn into one so it looked as though wind was flowing through it whenever Superman was supposed to be flying.

Along with the six capes, Reeve had 40 suits for the role. As he fought for truth, justice, and the American way, Superman never perspired or wrinkled. His clothes always had to look fresh. If Reeve began to sweat, he had to change his costume.

The suits posed another problem because they had no pockets. Reeve had to decide what to do with his hands when he wasn't flying or rescuing someone. His solution—folding his arms in front of him—served two purposes. In addition to occupying his hands, it made him look strong.

With his light brown hair dyed jet black, Reeve *looked* like a superhero, but could he actually *become* Superman? "I just played him as a friend," Reeve said. Sometimes the actor even treated the character as if he were a friend, calling him by the nickname "Supie" on the set.

More difficult than learning how to fly or understanding the thoughts of an alien, however, was the challenge of playing two different roles. Reeve thought of Superman and Clark Kent as two very different people. Kent was a disguise that Superman hid behind. In order to keep Superman's secret, Reeve had to make Kent seem so different that people would never suspect the truth. He didn't have to fool the audience, since they already knew Superman and Kent were the same person. But he did have to make it look as though he cared about fooling the make-believe world in the movie. He decided to slump his shoulders and hang his head when he played Clark Kent. That made the reporter appear to be three-and-a-half inches shorter than Superman. The two characters also walked and talked differently. While Kent seemed a bit shy and hesitant, Superman spoke and acted with assurance.

Just as Katharine Hepburn had advised him, Reeve brought himself into the roles to make each character distinct and believable. "Superman was me when I [was] most open, relaxed, friendly, poised and unself-conscious," he said. "When I played Clark Kent, I went to the other side of my character, the nervous, shy, clumsy, insecure guy who two years ago was trying to get a job and three years ago was trying to pick up a girl, neither with any success." On the set, Reeve also became the two characters he portrayed. "When I'm on the set as Clark Kent, I find this kind of mild-mannered meekness coming out in me," he told *Interview* magazine. "I might say, 'Umm, Mr. Donner, could I please maybe leave the set for uhh, ten minutes?' Then when I'm playing Superman, it's 'Alright

Reeve enjoyed playing the role of Clark Kent more than that of Superman.

over there, move it!' I don't give orders but I can feel a different kind of confidence, a different kind of energy."

Even though Superman may have made Reeve feel more powerful and confident, he preferred depicting Kent's insecurities. "In a funny way, Clark is more fun to play. There's more scope to the role because he is such an awful mess," he explained.

There's no doubt, though, that Reeve found it appealing to bring both sides of the comic book character to life. The internal struggles of Clark Kent may have drawn him to the part, but the dangerous side of Superman had its own attraction. "I believe that it is better to gamble, to go for high risk, than to stand around testing the water," he told a journalist while filming the movie. As a daredevil, he enjoyed the element of risk, but he also had the best interests of the movie in mind. As an actor, he wanted the director to be able to show Superman close up. That would not have been possible if a double had filled in.

Reeve hung 240 feet over Manhattan's East River, attached by a wire to a crane. He sometimes forgot that he was a mere mortal when he wore Superman's cape. "When I put on that costume I was dangerous—to myself," he remembered. "I used to think if the wires would break I'd keep going." During a scene with Margot Kidder, who played *The Daily Planet* reporter

Christopher Reeve and Margot Kidder make flying look realistic in Superman II.

Lois Lane, the rig that Kidder and Reeve were attached to began to crack. They were both dangerously dangling 30 feet in the air. Believing he possessed Superman's powers, Reeve reached out to try to catch Kidder. Luckily, crew members got them both down before anyone was hurt.

Because *Superman* required so much technical preparation for the special effects, the actors often had a great deal of spare time between takes. Reeve often wandered from department to department, asking crew members what they were doing and why they were doing it. He learned a little about editing, sound effects, and cameras. He often looked over director Richard Donner's shoulder and asked why he had chosen a particular lens or set up a scene in a certain way.

Reeve also made a new friend while filming *Superman*. In October 1977, he met Gae Exton, a British citizen and models' agent, in the Shepperton Studio cafeteria. "The first thing I noticed were those blue eyes," she said. "But it wasn't love at first sight." They did hit it off, however, and the couple moved in together four months later. Exton was in the middle of divorcing her millionaire husband, David Iveson.

Love and work didn't consume all of Reeve's time. He played the piano for 90 minutes each day. When he was on breaks from filming in New York City, he attended two plays on Sundays and one on Tuesday evenings.

The cast and crew finally completed all the footage for *Superman: The Movie*, but only part of the sequel

While filming Superman: The Movie *in England, Reeve met Gae Exton, a British citizen.*

was finished. Money had run out. Reeve said the first movie cost $30 million, although it's difficult to estimate since so much of *Superman II* was shot in conjunction with the original movie. Other estimates put the cost as high as $45 million and call the history-making motion picture the most expensive ever made up to that point. After 11 months of filming, Reeve was free to go back to his private life—and wait to see what the world thought of him in the role that had already made him famous.

Reeve's agents advised him against starring in the movie
Somewhere in Time. *He is shown here with costar Jane Seymour.*

Chapter **SIX**

TIME TRAVELER

CHRIS REEVE BROKE AWAY FROM A CONVERSATION he was having at a dinner party to celebrate the premiere of *Superman*. He reached out his right hand to Joe Shuster, one of the creators of the *Superman* comic books. "I can't believe it," Reeve said. "I just wanted to shake your hand."

Eunice Shriver, the founder of International Special Olympics, the wife of former vice presidential candidate Sargent Shriver, and a member of the politically famous Kennedy family, was hosting the party in her Rockville, Maryland, home. The party was just one of the weekend's several gala events surrounding the movie's premiere at Washington, D.C.'s John F. Kennedy Center for the Performing Arts on December 10, 1978.

Later that week, the movie was released in 700 theaters in English-speaking countries. While enthusiastic
audiences filled theaters to watch the two-hour-and-
fifteen-minute movie, critics praised the effort, and
many singled Reeve out. Although the *New York Times*
critic Vincent Canby said the movie had limited ap-
peal and didn't live up to the time and effort the producers had put into it, he praised Reeve's
performance. "In Christopher Reeve . . . the producers
and . . . director have a performer who manages to be
both funny and comic-strip heroic without making a
fool of himself," he wrote.

The movie became one of the five most successful
movies in history at that time. Other producers wanted
Reeve's star power to attract audiences to their movies,
and the actor was in a position to negotiate for higher
salaries. Scripts and movie offers began to come his
way, but Reeve was determined to choose his next role
based on the challenge it provided him as an actor. He
also wanted to avoid being typecast in parts similar to
that of Superman. "The next film, play, or whatever I
do I'll have to pick very carefully so I can break the
image right away," he declared.

One of the scripts his agents had passed on to him
was based on the novel *Bid Time Return* by Richard
Matheson. In the story, a dying man travels back in
time to 1912 to be with a stage actress whose photo
he has seen. Reeve agreed to meet with Stephen
Deutsch, the movie's producer, and Jeannot Szwarc,

the director. After the two men went to Reeve's home to discuss the script, Reeve thought, "I haven't seen anything like this in a long time." He found the main character, Richard Collier, especially appealing.

Reeve's agents advised him not to star in the movie version, *Somewhere in Time,* because they believed that the film wouldn't have a big audience or make much money. But Reeve decided for himself. "I do what I want and always have," he said. As much as he liked the script, he still had one request. He asked the moviemakers to rewrite the script so that Collier wouldn't be terminally ill. He believed the change would enable the viewers to identify with the character. When they agreed, he accepted $400,000 to play the starring role.

To prepare for the role of Collier, Reeve said, "What I need to do is to reawaken in myself the aspects of my life that are similar to him." Before filming began in the summer of 1979, Reeve moved from California back to the East Coast. To understand any character he played, Reeve thought about the character's hair color, clothes, and behavior, and then the actor attempted to alter himself to be like that character. To become Collier, Reeve eliminated junk food from his diet, because he thought the character was a healthy eater. He went through his closet and pulled out shirts and pants similar to ones Reeve thought Collier might wear. He also followed the same daily routine—waking, eating, and going out—that he thought Collier might follow. Since Collier is a playwright and writers work by themselves, Reeve isolated himself so he could understand a writer's feelings of loneliness.

After spending four days in Chicago to film the scenes set in 1980, the movie cast and crew moved to Mackinac Island, Michigan, to complete shooting. The actors, dressed in costumes from the early 20th century, transformed the lilac-covered island, which is located between Lakes Huron and Michigan.

Vehicles are not allowed on the island, but Universal, the studio making the picture, got permission to bring a camera and sound truck, a utility truck, and two

Somewhere in Time *was filmed on picturesque Mackinac Island in Michigan.*

vans for filming. Cast and crew members pedaled bicycles or rode in horse-drawn taxis.

Although the actors often worked six days a week, sometimes 16 hours each day, Sundays were their own. Reeve decided to spend one of his Sundays watching a special showing of *Superman* at the island's theater. Because of a technical problem, the movie stopped during the second reel. When the projectionist got the equipment rolling again, there was still no sound. To the audience's delight, Reeve began to recite the movie's dialogue from the third row until the sound returned.

On Sunday, July 3, Reeve and his costar, Jane Seymour, rode their bicycles to the island's airstrip with costumer Greg Hall and some of the movie's extras. Reeve piloted everyone off the island to go bowling in Petosky, Michigan. The actor needed the air miles to keep his pilot's license up to date, and this was a perfect excuse. Reeve later said, "It was a magical summer, where we just disappeared, reality was suspended, and it was very easy to insert ourselves into the world of the movie."

Reeve with Gae Exton and their first child, Matthew, who was born on December 20, 1979.

Chapter SEVEN

UPS AND DOWNS

CHRISTOPHER REEVE'S *SUPERMAN* SUCCESS EARNED him two honors from the acting community in 1979. Although he was not nominated for an award, the Academy of Motion Picture Arts and Sciences asked him to copresent the film editing Oscar at their March ceremony with actress Bo Derek. By making him a presenter, the film community acknowledged that Reeve had become a movie star.

The greatest honor that evening came when the curtain closed. Reeve stood between Cary Grant and John Wayne, two screen legends. "This is our new man," Grant said to Wayne, referring to Reeve. "He's taking over." Reeve was stunned and left speechless by the compliment.

On the other side of the Atlantic Ocean, Reeve had received a nomination for the British Academy Awards. In 1979, he won the Most Promising Newcomer award. He was undoubtedly an international success.

After Reeve had finished shooting *Somewhere in Time,* crews were ready to begin filming the sequel to *Superman.* Some of the *Superman II* scenes had been shot, but much work still remained. Then a problem arose. "When the producers looked at [the footage they had], they found most of it unacceptable," screenwriter David Newman explained. The Salkinds replaced Richard Donner with Richard Lester, who had directed the Beatles' first movie, *A Hard Day's Night.* Lester intended to shoot new scenes and reshoot parts of what Donner had completed.

Instead of using harnesses and wires, this time flight was simulated with a pole-on. "It's a system wherein a mold was taken of my body and that mold had a pole sticking out of the side of it," Sarah Douglas, the actor who portrayed villainous Ursa, explained. "The pole was attached to a screen of blue backing about forty feet off the ground." After the actors climbed into their molds from scaffolding, they put their costumes on, hiding the mold from sight. "When it came to *Superman II,* everyone worked a lot more on the special effects," Douglas said.

In the midst of the intense filming, Reeve had to start concentrating on another production. Gae Exton gave birth to their first child, Matthew, on

December 20, 1979. The proud father attended the delivery, but the next day he skied down the slopes of Switzerland, taking time off to relax before returning to *Superman II*'s grueling filming schedule. Exton said she didn't mind, since she understood that he had been exhausted from working and needed a break.

When Matthew was eight days old, Exton and the baby went with Reeve on location on the island of Barbados in the West Indies. "The important thing is to remain a family," Exton said. "Where his career leads, Matthew and I follow. My career can adjust. I consider myself a lucky girl."

Reeve was determined to be a good father and decided that he didn't want to raise his child in an unhappy home like the one he'd known as a child. "I'm not going to lay down the law," he said. "I can remember growing up thinking that one day I was going to have a kid or kids, and I wouldn't want them to go through what I did."

In March 1980, while back in England, Reeve found himself in the middle of an international incident. While he was flying his glider over the English countryside, his aircraft couldn't catch the air currents necessary to stay aloft. He crash-landed the glider in a British defense base. After Reeve touched down, defense officials arrested the intruder. Once they learned that the actor was no threat to national security, however, they treated him well. "We had tea and biscuits, and I wound up signing autographs," he said. Afterward, a British Defense Ministry spokesman joked, "It's not every day Superman drops in on us." Although Reeve wasn't injured in the incident, his ego suffered. "The newspapers heard about it and suggested I was a lousy pilot," he complained. "That upset me."

Directors and producers were sending Reeve about 12 scripts a week in early 1980. "Suddenly I was a big movie star sitting around Hollywood driving a Mercedes, . . . reading scripts, and I was beginning to hate myself," Reeve said. In order to regain his self-respect, Reeve returned to the Williamstown Theatre Festival, where he had made a splash 12 years earlier. Onstage before a live audience, he played serious dra-

Reeve took up gliding several years after he had learned to fly powered planes.

matic roles in two plays, *The Front Page* and *The Cherry Orchard*. That summer he earned $300 per week. When Reeve told his agent about his plans, the agent said, "Well, you'll get all that theater stuff out of your system." Instead, Reeve continued to return to Williamstown every summer he was able.

When *Somewhere in Time* premiered in October 1980, reviewers found the motion picture slow and plodding, and critics singled Reeve out as one of the movie's major problems. "[I]t's Mr. Reeve who sets the film's tone," wrote Vincent Canby in the *New York Times*. "Unfortunately, his unshadowed good looks, granite profile, bright naïveté and eagerness to please—the qualities that made him an ideal Superman—look absurd here." In New York's *Daily News*, Kathleen Carroll said, "Christopher Reeves (sic) may have flown in *Superman*, but as the hero of this tepid movie, he appears to have trouble simply putting one foot in front of the other." His second starring role had been an unqualified failure.

Reeve didn't seem concerned that his film career had taken a downturn, however. He loved the stage and was eager to return to live theater. On November 5, 1980, *Fifth of July* opened at the Circle Repertory Theater in New York City.

In the play, Reeve portrayed Kenneth Talley Jr., a homosexual paraplegic. As usual, he researched the part thoroughly, learning about the physical and emotional demands on someone in the character's situation.

"I trained with a real paraplegic who had his legs blown off in Vietnam," Reeve said. "He showed me how to use artificial legs, how to walk with arm braces, but even more he taught me the meaning of *optimism.*"

Even with intense research, however, Reeve wasn't prepared when it was time for the preview performance in front of an audience. "We only had seventeen days of rehearsal before the first preview, and when we opened we really were not ready," he explained. Critics attend performances called previews before a show actually opens so that their review can appear when the play opens. The reviewers were unimpressed by the movie star. "The critics said I was wooden, and they were right," he agreed.

Reeve continued in the role for seven months, however, and by the time he finished, he was proud of the way he had portrayed Kenneth Talley. "It really is the thing I'm proudest of in my career so far," he said.

Reeve played opposite Swoosie Kurtz and Amy Wright in the Broadway play Fifth of July.

Christopher Reeve, far right in the back row, **with the 1980 Williamstown Theatre Festival company**

Fifth of July may have helped the world forget about *Superman* for a while, but when *Superman II* came out in June 1981, once again the audience thought Reeve, Superman, and Clark Kent were practically the same person. One critic raved, "Mr. Reeve is so perfectly suited to the Superman role that he gives the film a warmth and energy it might not otherwise have. Mr. Reeve's Clark Kent is even better."

Reeve believes that the first two *Superman* movies enabled him to earn a starring Broadway role ten years faster than he would have without the film. "Without *Superman,* I'd still be a struggling actor, doing it the hard way," he said. "I know that, and I'm very grateful for that movie stardom. But it's time to do something else." That summer he returned to Williamstown Theatre Festival to portray Achilles in *The Greeks.*

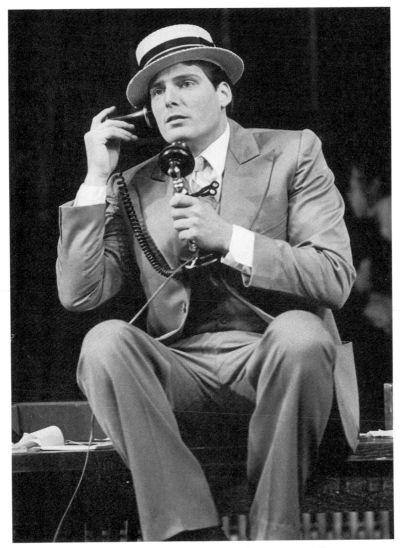

Reeve acted in The Front Page *during the 1980 Williamstown Theatre Festival. He enjoyed the live stage.*

Chapter **EIGHT**

SUPERMAN CAN ACT!

BY THE SUMMER OF **1981,** GAE WAS WORKING four days each week as a model. A Scottish *au pair,* a live-in babysitter, cared for Matthew when his parents worked. When they weren't working, however, they focused their attention on their young son. "The key to being a good father is never to think you own your child—you don't," Reeve said.

Reeve played the role of his life in the family's penthouse on the Upper West Side of New York City. He spent time with Matthew and helped Gae tend their rooftop garden.

To the people they socialized with, the fact that they had never wed was not important. "We're a couple in everyone's eyes—I think most people have forgotten we're not married," Gae said. She was happy with the arrangement, explaining, "Having been married once, I'm in no hurry to do it again." Reeve echoed her statement. "Gae and I are very happy the way we are."

With Reeve's family life in order, he carefully planned his career. After the success of *Superman II*, Reeve set out once again to prove that he was a versatile actor. In his next film, *Deathtrap*, he portrayed Clifford Anderson, a young psychopathic playwright. His former teacher, Sidney Bruhl, played by Michael Caine, is a well-known playwright who has recently had a series of flops. Together Anderson and Bruhl

Reeve played a psychopathic playwright in the movie Deathtrap.

Sidney Lumet, who had been nominated for several Oscars, directed Deathtrap.

murder Bruhl's wife. Anderson then decides to write a play about their scheme and murder Bruhl.

The part appealed to Reeve for several reasons. He liked the script and found the opportunity to play such a character "a nice acting challenge." He also welcomed the chance to work with the movie's director, Sidney Lumet. Lumet had been an Oscar nominee for his directorial work on *The Verdict, Network,* and *Dog Day Afternoon*. He cast Reeve in *Deathtrap* partly because of his performance in *Fifth of July.* "It was just thrilling to see what he did with that role," Lumet said. "There was real courage evident in him as an actor."

Reeve's next film, Monsignor, was released in October 1982.

The collaboration paid off. Although the film did not make a lot of money at the box office when it was released in March 1982, the actor's and director's styles meshed. "Sidney Lumet works by being part camp counselor, part psychiatrist and part technical director," Reeve told a journalist. "You simply walk into a world in which he is a benevolent dictator and you trust yourself completely—like those exercises where people stand backwards on a table and fall off trusting the group will catch them." The feeling was mutual. Lumet said that Reeve "was always an arresting talent and did first-class work from the beginning."

In Reeve's next film, *Monsignor*, which opened in movie theaters in October 1982, Reeve portrayed Father John Flaherty, a Roman Catholic priest who commited heresy—including having an affair with a nun—while scheming to raise money for the Vatican. To understand the responsibilities and commitment required of a priest, Reeve attended a special retreat before going off to Rome, Italy, to film the movie. Men who had studied to become priests attended the retreat in order to think about their decision before taking their vows. "At first I felt very out of place among these people who had made a real strong choice about their commitment," he said. But eventually, the actor felt more at ease and took part in prayer and discussions about religion. He also learned how to say a mass in Latin and how to give communion.

In Superman III, *the hero temporarily turned evil. The movie also added a humorous element that had been absent from the first two versions.*

Vanessa Redgrave, seated center, *and Christopher Reeve,* far left, *chat with director James Ivory,* right, *on the set of* The Bostonians.

Although Reeve kept saying he wanted to leave his Superman image behind, he found it difficult to do. With the release of *Superman III* in June 1983, Reeve was once again flying across movie screens. Directed by Richard Lester and filmed in Alberta, Canada, this installment differed from the first two. Comedian Richard Pryor joined the cast and added a humorous element. Lois Lane was no longer the only woman in the dual life of Superman and Clark Kent. *The Daily Planet's* new boss, Lacy Warfield, who was played by Mariel Hemingway, and Lana Lang, played by Annette O'Toole, tried to woo the superhero-reporter. The most significant change, however, was that Superman

Gae Exton, shown here with Christopher and Matthew, gave birth to a daughter, Alexandra, in December 1983.

temporarily turned evil. In the final outcome, of course, the good Superman triumphed in a battle with his evil self.

Reeve had called the third movie the "ultimate comic book," but he promised that the world had seen the last of him in tights and a cape. "I've flown, become evil, loved, stopped and turned the world backward," he explained. "I've faced my peers, I've befriended children and small animals and I've rescued cats from trees. What is there left for Superman to do that hasn't been done?"

When *The Bostonians* screened at the Cannes Film Festival in May 1984, Reeve finally proved to the world that he was a serious actor. "[A] ripple of amazement could be heard throughout the theater: 'Superman can act!' was the recurring refrain," Annette Insdorf wrote in the *New York Daily News* before the movie's August release. The character's moral complexity drew Reeve to the Basil Ransome role of a 19th-century Mississippi lawyer battling for the love of a charismatic lecturer who promotes women's rights. Reeve believed Ransome was either a chauvinist pig or a genuine romantic trying to save the heroine from what he viewed as a bland existence. Reeve liked the contradictory elements.

Reeve also liked working with the director, James Ivory. Reeve said Ivory and Lumet were the best movie

Reeve flew to Yugoslavia for the filming of The Aviator.

directors he's worked with. Although the studio did not think Reeve was right for the part, Ivory insisted. "Jim Ivory said that he cast me because of the work I had done in *Superman*, not in spite of it," Reeve said. That was not the only reason he enjoyed this movie-making experience. He also appreciated Ivory's directorial style—gathering ideas about a scene from the entire cast. "Then he rationally takes the best of everyone's offerings," Reeve explained.

The Bostonians also gave Reeve the opportunity to work with Vanessa Redgrave, a renowned British actor. Although he was often intimidated by her intensity and professionalism, he says that those qualities brought out the best in him.

In December 1983, Gae gave birth to their daughter,

Morgan Freeman and Christopher Reeve in Street Smart

Alexandra. Once again, Reeve flew back from his filming location to London to be with her. When Gae had become pregnant with their second child, gossip columnists began to report that she wasn't happy with her marital status. According to them, she had threatened to leave Reeve if the couple was not married by the time the child was born. After Matthew was born, she had stated, "One illegitimate child is fine, but two is, well, tacky." She was ready to marry her children's father, but he was unable to commit.

While Gae decided what to do about her situation, Reeve flew to Yugoslavia for the filming of his next movie, *The Aviator*, which turned out to be a box office disaster. Nearly two years after Alexandra's birth, Reeve and Exton were still together. In fact, Reeve said he considered their London town house to be his real home. But Reeve didn't mention Gae or the children when he explained why he called London home. Instead, he remarked that he liked life in England because he was not as well known there as he was in the United States.

In September 1985, Menachem Golan and Yoram Globus, who headed a company called Cannon Pictures Group, asked Reeve to star in *Superman IV*. The studio had purchased the movie rights from Warner Brothers. Reeve agreed under three conditions: that he write the script for the *Superman* sequel; that he star in *Street Smart*, a script he had first read in 1981; and that he get $4 million for his work on the films. Cannon agreed to the terms.

In *Street Smart,* Reeve plays Jonathan Fisher, a journalist who is so desperate to write an important article for a weekly New York magazine that he makes up a story about New York City crime. The story boomerangs when the district attorney concludes the article is about a real-life murder suspect. To research the part, Reeve followed a magazine writer and some New York City undercover police officers while they worked.

When *Street Smart* filmed in Toronto, Canada, and New York City, Gae took time off from her work in London. She and the children followed Chris, living in their Upper West Side apartment, then flying back to England. He was lucky to have his family near him. While filming in June 1986, Reeve had to be rushed to Roosevelt Hospital in New York City for an emergency appendectomy. The operation and recuperation delayed the film schedule for about four days.

When the movie came out in March 1987, Reeve suffered another box office disappointment. In the *Wall Street Journal,* movie critic Julie Salamon panned the motion picture, saying, "Mr. Reeve is the main problem but not the only one." The movie wasn't a total failure, however, since costar Morgan Freeman received an Oscar nomination for his role.

While skiing in Vermont, Reeve thought up the plot for *Superman IV: The Quest for Peace.* He began working on the script, which is about ridding the world of nuclear weapons, in December 1985. "What I did

Gene Hackman with Christopher Reeve in Superman IV.

particularly enjoy on this one was saying, 'Okay what would I like to see the character do?'" Reeve said. "It would be nice to see a *Superman* movie from his point of view." He began getting in shape for the role in August 1986, and the cameras rolled the following month in England's Elstree Studios.

That same summer, Reeve bought a 40-acre home in Massachusetts near the New York border, with "a cross-country ski run, livestock, trout stream, and a pond." He said he purchased the home so that he could park his glider but admitted that he had other plans for the new residence, too. At last he was talking about marrying his long-time girlfriend. "I figured I'll rebuild the house until it's large and perfect enough for our wedding," he explained. "By then our son Matthew, who's now seven, will be old enough to be Best Man at his parent's marriage, and three-year-old Alexandra can be our flower girl."

Even this idyllic home couldn't keep the couple together, however. In fact, Reeve's fantasy wedding was just an attempt to fool the public. By February 1987, Reeve and Exton had finally ended their relationship. Gae never actually lived in the house with Reeve. Instead Chris's half brothers, Jeff and Kevin, found work in the area and moved in. Chris's professional life took an unpleasant downturn, too.

Although Reeve had more control over this movie than any other, *Superman IV*'s July 1987 release disappointed the actor, and he regretted having made the picture. Reeve thought the studio was working on too many films at once and couldn't give the third *Superman* sequel the attention it needed.

That summer Reeve managed to get someone else's attention, however. During his season at the Williamstown Theatre Festival, Dana Morosini, a 26-year-old actor and singer, performed one evening— June 30, 1987—at a cabaret in town. Enraptured by her beautiful voice and face, Chris watched her sing "The Music That Makes Me Dance" from the musical *Funny Girl*. After the performance, he went backstage and introduced himself.

Reeve met actor and singer Dana Morosini during the 1987 Williamstown Theatre Festival.

Morosini and Reeve ran into each other a few days later. When they sat down to talk, "everything just vanished around us," Reeve said. They had a lot to talk about. Dana also enjoyed sailing, skiing, and horseback riding, a sport that Reeve had just begun that year, since his former allergies had vanished. Reeve showered his new girlfriend with flowers and cards. "It was a very old-fashioned courtship," Dana explained. "He'd come over to watch me rehearse. He'd pick wildflowers and have them carried over by an apprentice." They started dating and then moved in together six months later.

While his personal life was taking off, Reeve's film career was fizzling. He continued to act onstage, but appearances in TV movies and specials accounted for most of his work. Unfortunately, television roles do not pay as well as movie roles.

Reeve's personal life took a new direction, too. On a December evening in 1991, four-and-a-half years after Dana and Chris met, they were enjoying a romantic candlelight dinner in their Manhattan penthouse.

Chris and Dana with Matthew and Alexandra, Reeve's children by Gae Exton

Suddenly, they both looked at each other and said, "Let's get married." In a small ceremony on April 11, 1992, they exchanged vows they had written themselves. Matthew was Reeve's best man, and Alexandra was Morosini's maid of honor.

On June 7 that year, Chris welcomed his third child when Dana gave birth to their son, Will, in North Adams, Massachusetts, near Williamstown. Although he suffered from colic during the first months of his life, Will seemed to enjoy the activity whirling around him. Matthew and Alexandra spent the summer with their father and took turns caring for their half brother. Reeve occasionally put Will in a backpack carrier and took him for a hike in the mountains. At night he gave Will a bath.

By the end of November 1992, Reeve had finished the shooting of *The Remains of the Day*, his second movie under James Ivory's direction. Earlier that year, Reeve had attended the premiere of *Howards End*, also directed by Ivory. When the film ended, Reeve told the director, "Any part in your next movie, please." Ivory remembered the request and soon sent the actor a script with a note that said, "You're Lewis."

Playing the part gave Reeve the opportunity to work with Emma Thompson and Anthony Hopkins, two renowned Academy Award-winning actors. "I had an Oscar on my right, an Oscar on my left. Suddenly Superman didn't feel so super," he joked about the experience.

Working with such talented actors had a positive effect on Reeve's performance. When the film was released in November 1993, critics praised Ivory and the cast. Many reviewers said the acting was outstanding and the work was Ivory's best ever. *Variety* magazine's critic Todd McCarthy wrote, "Reeve brings authority and Yankee energy" to his role. Reeve described his performance in the movie as his most natural. It also marked his last high-profile movie role.

Reeve played a paralyzed policeman in *Above Suspicion*, his final role before his horseback riding accident. The television movie aired on the Home Box Office (HBO) cable network. Reeve researched the part at a spinal-cord trauma unit in Van Nuys, California, after the area had been hit by a major earthquake. Many of the patients had had bookcases fall on them as their homes shook in the quake. "You see how easily it could happen," he said about the visits. "You think, God, it could happen to anybody."

Reeve's remarkable rehabilitation and his determination to find a cure for victims of spinal cord injuries have spurred new research in the field.

Chapter NINE

SMALL STEPS

WHEN THE HELICOPTER *PEGASUS* TOUCHED DOWN
at the University of Virginia Medical Center on
May 27, 1995, medics quickly transported Reeve into
the hospital's emergency room. Dr. Mohan Nadkami,
the doctor in charge of the ER, and his staff quickly
began procedures to save the actor's life. First, they
slid Reeve's body onto a bed with a halo to secure his
head and weights to hold him down. Although he was
paralyzed and could not consciously move, his muscles involuntarily reacted in spasms, causing him to
jerk his head from side to side or flail. An injection of
morphine sedated him. Once Reeve was stable, Dr.
Nadkami—or "Dr. Mo" as the Reeves later called
him—amused Will while Dana sat by her husband's

bedside. Reeve remained connected to a respirator since he still could not breathe on his own.

Soon other family members learned about the accident and traveled to Charlottesville to join Dana. Gae, 15-year-old Matthew, and 11-year-old Alexandra arrived with Reeve's mother. Reeve's father came from Connecticut, and his brother, Ben, traveled from Massachusetts to see him.

For four days, Reeve's condition stayed the same. He didn't awake, and he ate through a feeding tube. Dana sat by his bed, singing comforting songs, such as "Amazing Grace" and "Peace in the Valley." Then on Wednesday, May 31, Reeve woke up. Unable to speak, he mouthed questions to his family. "He was asking what had happened," Barbara Johnson explained. "It was tough. You could see him struggling." He had no recollection of the accident.

Reeve learned that surgeons would have to operate to repair his spine. He had developed pneumonia, however, a common complication for paralysis patients because they must lie flat. The doctors couldn't proceed with surgery until his lungs cleared up. Reeve also learned that he had a 50 percent chance of survival and that he could die during the operation. After the doctors left and the dismal prospect of recovery sank in, Reeve mouthed words to Dana, suggesting that it might be better just to let him die. Without hesitating, Dana stared into his eyes and said, "But you're still you, and I love you." And when Matthew, Alexandra,

Dr. John Jane, professor of neurosurgery at the University of Virginia Medical Center, held a press conference to describe Reeve's medical condition.

and Will stepped into the room he asked himself, "How can I possibly leave them?"

Until this point, the Reeve family had asked the hospital not to reveal information about Chris's condition to the public or media. Finally, the family decided they could be more open with the press and issued formal statements. Reeve's doctor, John Jane, a specialist in trauma injuries, revealed what he knew about the actor's medical condition. He explained that Reeve had broken his spine at the top between the first and second vertebrae—also called C1 and C2. He then added that Reeve could not move or breathe on his own.

While Dr. Jane handled the medical report, the Reeve family's statement was more personal. "[W]e do not know what lies ahead," they stated in writing. "It means everything to Christopher and his family to have all of your thoughts and prayers."

On behalf of the family, Benjamin Reeve delivered a personal message about his brother's condition.

Mail began to pour into the hospital, including letters from President Bill Clinton and Pope John Paul II. Children colored pictures, and spinal cord injury patients wrote encouraging letters. Gifts and flowers overwhelmed the mailroom. Volunteers helped the family open and sort the cards and letters, and the Reeves distributed the flowers to other patients.

Alexandra wrote to a third-grade Charlottesville class that had sent cards and drawings. "My dad's very sick, and that is why I am writing to you, not him," she explained. "But I have told him about your letters, and he is very grateful."

By Friday the family had good news. The patient had some feeling in his chest. Sensation below the neck meant that the break hadn't been complete and that part of the spine around the break had not been damaged. In addition to the physical progress, Reeve had made emotional progress, too. Ben reported that his brother had regained his sense of humor.

By June 5, the pneumonia had cleared up enough to operate. At 8:30 A.M. the procedure began. In addition to Dr. Jane, Scott Henson, the hospital's chief resident for neurosurgery, and Chris Shaffrey, the orthopedic spine specialist, performed the operation. The doctors put a wire under Reeve's lamina, the boney covering over the spinal cord, placed bone from his hip between C1 and C2, then stitched the vertebrae together. Certain that the bond was solid, they fused 11 titanium metal rings to the wire under the lamina. With the rings in place, the surgeons drilled holes into the base of Reeve's skull and passed wires through those, essentially reattaching his head to his spine. The complicated procedure ended at 3:00 P.M.

Later that day, Dr. Jane announced, "Everything went well. I am confident [Reeve] will be stable." The patient was able to nod and move his head from side to side and sit at a 30-degree angle with assistance. On June 7, the hospital revealed that Reeve could move his right shoulder muscle. He could also eat solid food with someone else's help.

Dana made her first public statement two days later. She hinted at what she had been going through since the accident. "[T]his has to be the toughest challenge he has ever faced," she said. "I know it is mine." But she was also lighthearted. After explaining that Chris saw his children, parents, and brother every day and watched hockey on TV, she joked, "I think his spirits might be better if the Rangers were in the playoffs."

Robin Williams, who was on a break from filming *The Birdcage*, came to Charlottesville to see his friend on June 9. Wearing a blue scrub hat and yellow gown, he pushed a wheelchair into Reeve's room. He spoke with a Russian accent, insisting the paralyzed patient get out of the bed and into the chair. Because Williams was hanging upside down, Reeve couldn't see his friend's face, but Reeve knew only one person had that kind of sense of humor. The spoof gave Reeve his first laugh after the accident.

Although Reeve could sit up for 30 minutes by June 13, he still couldn't breathe without a ventilator. To check the effort his muscles were making as he tried to take in air, Reeve breathed into an NIF—a negative inspiratory force. The machine was supposed to register his score on a dial, but he was unable to move the dial. Eventually, he gave up. Then one day, he declared, "I'm going to breathe. I've got to make some progress here." He took 10 breaths and managed to make the dial move. His first words without the respirator were, "Testing—one, two, three."

Although Reeve made some progress nearly every day, the nights were often excruciating. "Down in Virginia, it wasn't so much fun at first, because I would wake up at two in the morning and stare out the window and feel fairly sorry for myself," he said. Nothing could eliminate the sorrow, but to help improve his spirits, Reeve would look at a photo on the wall of his room. The photo was of a Buddhist temple with many steps leading up to the blue sky overhead. The small

A photo of this Buddhist temple hung on a wall in Reeve's hospital room. The steps on the temple became a symbol of his rehabilitation.

steps leading to the goal at the end became a symbol of Reeve's rehabilitation. He would take small steps to reach his goal. For Reeve, that goal was walking.

Reeve began the next phase of recovery at the Kessler Institute in West Orange, New Jersey. The Reeves had chosen Kessler because of its impressive rehabilitation program and the fact that it was only three hours from their home. The University of Virginia Medical Center discharged Christopher Reeve at 9:00 A.M. on June 28, 1995. In fog and pouring rain, Chris, Will, and Dana flew to Morristown, New Jersey, and then rode in an ambulance to the Kessler Institute.

Marcalee Sipski, director of the spinal cord unit, was in charge of Reeve's rehabilitation at the new hospital. But Reeve was not yet ready to begin the demanding workouts that would allow his body to function again. At the University of Virginia, his weight had dropped from 215 to 190 pounds. His protein levels were low, and he was not eating well.

Although Reeve's physical condition certainly held him back from rehabilitation, his mental state also played a part. He isolated himself from the other patients, preferring to stay in his private room with two security guards outside at all times.

Reeve's concerns weren't all in his head, however. Only a week after arriving at the rehabilitation center, his doctors decided to give him Sygen, an experimental drug for spinal cord injuries. Medical researchers believed that the drug might have positive effects on

Reeve. Instead, he had an allergic reaction. As his heart beat faster, his blood pressure dropped, and he stopped breathing. One of Reeve's doctors, Steven Kirshblum, rushed into the room and injected him with epinephrine. A few minutes later, his breathing was back to normal.

Although Reeve had good reasons to be anxious, one day he suddenly decided to take control. He began to read about his injury and its complications. Then he decided he didn't need security guards anymore, and he left his room to meet other patients. He also kept track of his progress.

Of course, Reeve's family also played an important role in his rehabilation. Dana visited Chris every day,

Matthew and Alexandra visited their father frequently while he was hospitalized.

driving three hours each way, and Exton often brought Matthew and Alexandra to the hospital. When the older children eventually had to return to England, Reeve used his computer to communicate with them. AM Technologies had given him a software program that recognized his voice and followed his commands. "I can work on the Internet and send E-mail," he said. "I can talk to my two older kids in England, where they go to school. I ask them how their day was, and play chess with Matthew. It's good fun."

Reeve's wheelchair frightened him at first. "My arms were strapped down," he explained. "A seat belt was

At a 1997 speech in Milwaukee, Wisconsin, Reeve urged an audience of 16,000 not to look away when they are faced with someone with a handicap.

put on me. My legs were strapped onto foot pedals. It was like being put in an electric chair." Eventually, he learned to steer the Quickie P300 by blowing into an air tube. Depending on how long he exhaled, he moved the chair forward or backward, to the right or the left, quickly or slowly.

In September, Dr. Sipski agreed that Reeve could celebrate his birthday at home. He and Dana had purchased the house the year they got married so he'd be able to ride horses on the seven surrounding acres. Now he couldn't do that. "[A]t first I was thrilled to see the house and everything the way it was," Reeve said, "and then I just broke down because you realize how much everything has changed and how you are going to be different in the house and how everyone is going to have to make so many changes to accommodate this new life."

The house was in the midst of preparations for Reeve's permanent return. A new master bedroom for Chris and Dana had to be constructed on the first floor, since Reeve could no longer climb the stairs to get to the old one on the second floor. The sunken living room also had to be raised and the steps that led to it eliminated. The garage was being converted to a gym for Reeve's rehabilitation.

Reeve traveled away from Kessler again on October 16, 1995. Although his doctors had advised him not to attend the event, he rode in his van to the Pierre Hotel in Manhattan to present Robin Williams with the Cre-

Before his accident, Reeve had helped form the Creative Coalition, an organization that supports various social causes, and he had been an active lobbyist.

ative Coalition Spotlight Award. Reeve had helped found the organization, which supports a variety of social causes, including actors' rights. At a special reception preceding the ceremony, Reeve and Williams joked and reminisced about their days at Juilliard. Reeve greeted friends, colleagues, and politicians. At the ceremony, 700 people stood and cheered when Reeve was wheeled onstage. When Robin Williams joined him, the two actors joked about the wheelchair and Reeve's stylish new necktie—his breathing tube.

When he returned to Kessler, Reeve worked harder than ever. For inspiration he hung a poster signed by every NASA astronaut at that time. Next to a picture of a space shuttle taking off were the words, "We found nothing is impossible." Reeve took the words to heart. He had made very little progress on his breathing. His doctors had essentially given up on improvement, since Reeve hadn't tried to breathe without the ventilator since May. Reeve insisted on trying again in early November. For the first three days, he got better and better, then on the fourth day, he breathed off the ventilator for seven minutes. His therapists said they had never seen such progress so quickly.

Reeve, his wife, Dana, and actor Robin Williams pose at the Governor's Ball after the 68th Annual Academy Awards presentations.

Christopher Reeve was greeted with a standing ovation when he appeared at the Academy Awards ceremony in 1996.

Chapter **TEN**

THE
HOMECOMING

ON DECEMBER 13, 1995, REEVE RETURNED
home to continue his rehabilitation. By that time, he
no longer needed a feeding tube, and he could breathe
on his own for 15 minutes at a time. The change of
atmosphere worked wonders on him mentally and
physically. When one of his doctors visited for a
checkup, his blood pressure, oxygen levels, and blood
and protein counts had all improved.

During the night, nurses flip Reeve every three or
four hours from one side to the other so he doesn't
rest in one position too long, causing sores to develop
on his skin. While he sleeps, someone monitors his
respirator to make sure it doesn't run out of batteries
or become detached.

Reeve awakes at 7:30 A.M. and eats a breakfast of fruit before beginning his one to three hours of physical therapy. His workouts include breathing and neck exercises, riding his StimMaster bike, and working on the tilt table. While he exercises on the bicycle, he wears special pants with electrodes attached. The electrodes send a 50-volt current into his muscles, causing them to contract and expand. This portion of his physical therapy works his leg muscles. Because the stimulation allows him to pedal the bike, Reeve also gets an aerobic workout.

About twice a week, Reeve is strapped to the tilt table, a device that allows him to stand at a 70-degree angle with his legs and feet supporting his full body weight. He generally remains upright for about one hour. He also goes through a series of muscle-toning exercises with his therapist, who pushes his leg off to the side, up to the chest, and straight up. Since Reeve can't feel anything, he often stares out the window at the pond, goats, sheep, and guinea hens. The purpose of the therapy is to keep Reeve's muscles in shape to walk again.

To make that dream come true, Reeve founded the Reeve-Irvine Research Center, which is dedicated to finding a cure for spinal cord injury. Reeve announced on January 10, 1996, that Joan Irvine Smith had donated $1 million to the center, part of the College of Medicine at the University of California in Irvine. In addition to researching a cure for people who suffer nerve damage, the center encourages doctors who participate in such research to cooperate with one another in the effort to find a cure. Smith, who loves horses, had seen Reeve interviewed on television by Barbara Walters the previous September. She appreciated the fact that Reeve had never blamed his horse Buck for his injuries. The California government matched the grant, so Reeve had $2 million to begin his new center.

Although Reeve experienced many successes, he also had some difficult days. On January 16, 1996, for example, he suffered an excruciating headache. "You know what an ice-cream headache feels like? Take that and multiply it 20 or 30 times," he said about the unbearable pain. The headache was a sign that he had developed autonomic dysreflexia, a condition that many spinal cord injury patients get. These patients are easily constipated, and Reeve's blocked bowel had led to a urinary tract infection. His blood pressure soared so high that he and his caregivers worried that he might have a heart attack or stroke. He checked into Northern Westchester Hospital Center for six days so that the infection could be treated.

By early February, Reeve was breathing off the respirator for 90 minutes at a time. His ability to move his shoulder had increased, and although he was still unable to move his left leg on his own, 75 percent of it had sensation.

The world saw Reeve for the first time after the accident when he made a surprise appearance at the 68th Annual Academy Awards in Los Angeles on March 25, 1996. When the show's producer, music legend Quincy Jones, first called Reeve to ask him to appear, the actor said he'd think about the request. By the end of the call, however, Reeve had agreed. His doctors said he was stable enough to fly, and they approved the trip. Although Reeve wasn't absolutely sure it was a good idea to make the journey, he considered the appearance another challenge to overcome. "I don't mean to be reckless, but setting a goal that seems a bit daunting actually is very helpful to recovery," he said.

After two months of secretive planning, the show's organizers flew him across the country with Dana and five doctors. He appeared to a standing ovation to introduce a segment on movies with social themes. Moved by the audience's reaction, he told the *Los Angeles Times,* "After a long time in a rehab center and at home, kept in by snowstorms, it was very liberating and uplifting to be welcomed back in that way." Because he had wanted his words to carry personal meaning, he wrote the text himself. His appearance brought the audience to tears.

Inspired by his warm Oscar reception, Reeve continued to leave his home, becoming an outspoken activist for spinal cord injury research funding. He had always believed that celebrities bore a social responsibility, and Reeve had often lobbied the U.S. Congress for laws to protect the environment and guarantee the rights of artists. This time, he returned to Washington to ask for money to find a cure for spinal cord injury. On May 13, he hosted a reception for the Dana Alliance for Brain Initiatives, a group that raises money for SCI research.

In a meeting with President Bill Clinton on May 15, 1996, the president allocated $10 million to the National Institutes of Health (NIH) for spinal cord injury research. The NIH conducts medical research and provides money to other medical research organizations. When Reeve heard the news, he asked President Clinton, "Don't you want to announce that?" Clinton responded, "No, you go ahead." As television cameras rolled and reporters looked on, Reeve made the announcement in front of about 15 members of Congress, including Senators Paul Simon, Patrick Leahy, Paul Wellstone, and Nancy Kassebaum and Representative Jack Kemp—all of whom he considered friends. When Arlen Specter, the chair of the NIH funding subcommittee, heard about the president's commitment, he agreed that Congress would also support increased funding.

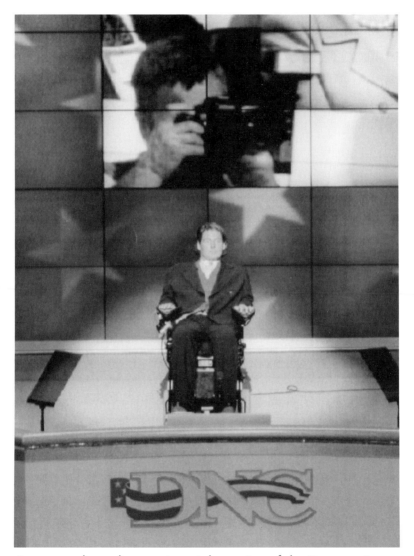

Reeve speaks to the opening night session of the Democratic National Convention in Chicago, Illinois, on August 26, 1996.

Chapter **ELEVEN**

A New Chapter

ON **AUGUST 26, 1996, REEVE MADE AN IM-**
passioned speech at the Democratic National
Convention in Chicago, as politicians, state delegates,
First Lady Hillary Rodham Clinton, and Dana
watched from the gallery. Reeve told the crowd that
about 250,000 people have a spinal cord injury and
that the government spends $8.7 billion to take care
of them, "but we spend only $40 million on research
that would actually improve the quality of their lives,
get them off the public dole, or even cure them. We
have got to be smarter and do better," he said. "The
money we invest in research today is going to determine the quality of life of members of our family
tomorrow."

With the spotlight shining down on him, Reeve told the audience about Gregory Patterson, who had been shot in the neck by a stray bullet from a gang shooting while he was innocently driving through Newark, New Jersey. "Today, because of research he is alive," Reeve said. "But . . . merely being alive is not enough. We have a moral and an economic responsibility to ease his suffering and to prevent others from experiencing such pain." He added that we don't have to raise taxes to accomplish that goal. Instead, we need to raise our expectations. He meant that the initiative would not cost citizens any more, but government money could be spent in better ways than was currently being done.

Reeve lent an important voice to the effort to raise funds for spinal cord injury research. The American Paralysis Association (APA) reported dramatic increases in interest in the topic and funding for research since the actor joined the fight. But Reeve was not interested in full-time activism. He craved the opportunity to work again. He got his chance when Michael Fuchs, the former head of the Home Box Office (HBO) cable company, visited him in early April 1996 with the perfect script. *In the Gloaming* is a story about a family whose adult son develops AIDS and returns to his parents' home to die.

Colin Callander, HBO NYC Productions' executive vice president, visited Reeve in early May. "When I sat down with Chris for the first time, I was struck by

Dana, left, *and Alexandra,* right, *with Reeve at a private screening of* In the Gloaming

how relevant this was to his own situation," Callander remarked. In the story, the entire family must adjust to having the patient there with his nurse and all of his other special needs, just as Reeve's family had done. After Callander decided they could work out the issues of how Chris would direct from a wheelchair, he signed him up for his directorial debut.

Rehearsals began in mid-September 1996, and shooting proceeded the following week. Reeve filmed the movie in a Pound Ridge, New York, home only ten minutes from his house. The company dubbed themselves "The Pound Ridge Players" because, in addition to Reeve, many cast and crew members lived in the area.

From 10:00 A.M. to 7:00 P.M., every weekday for one month, the crew made technical adjustments, the cameras rolled, the cast performed, and Reeve directed. The *whooshing* of his ventilator would have distracted the actors and ruined the sound track, so Reeve directed from a room that came to be known as "Video Village." He sat in his chair in front of monitors—television screens that let him see everything through the eyes of the cameraman. The cameraman had a viewfinder that transmitted directly to Reeve's monitor, and they used microphones and speakers to communicate, just as if Reeve were on the set. The monitors allowed Reeve to see the action elsewhere on the set. Chris spoke to camera operators through a headset and to the actors through a microphone. When he needed to meet with performers privately, he called them into the monitor room. Except for the fact that his personal assistant, Nick Childs, had to put the headset on Reeve and adjust the volume of his microphone, his experience really wasn't very different from that of other directors.

The new director could also share his acting knowledge with the cast of veteran actors. "Chris would tell us, 'if you cry too much, the audience won't cry with you. So hold back until you can't,'" Close explained. "It was incredibly helpful advice." Reeve also impressed Close with the way he treated the cast and crew, always showing his appreciation for their work.

Reeve loved the chance to be behind the scenes rather than in front of the camera. "The wonderful thing about directing is I'm energized all day long. I get to make decisions all day, and I find that really satisfying." Actors often have to wait while the director and costars shoot other scenes or the technical crew makes adjustments. As a director, Reeve never took a break.

By the end of October 1996, Reeve was in the editing room, splicing the film into its final cut. After he put the finishing touches on the motion picture, he delivered it to HBO on time and under budget. Pleased with the director's first effort, the network scheduled an April 20, 1997, television debut, which would follow a private screening and reception at the Museum of Modern Art on Monday, April 7.

Glenn Close poses with Reeve at the premiere of In the Gloaming, *a television movie that Reeve directed.*

Reeve and Dana smile as he receives a standing ovation from the audience at a fund-raising concert for the Christopher Reeve Foundation held at the McCarter Theatre in 1997.

Reeve nearly missed his first premiere as a director, however. On April 5, the nurse and the aide lifting him from his exercise bike to his wheelchair miscalculated each others' maneuvers. Reeve ended up on the edge of his chair, then fell over the side of the chair and onto the floor, landing on his left arm.

The next morning he and Dana went to Northern Westchester for an X ray, which indicated that the bone between Reeve's shoulder and elbow, the humerus, had broken in two. Instead of realigning the bones and putting a cast on Reeve's arm, the doctors operated. He lost four pints of blood during the procedure, but he was home three hours later.

At the Monday evening screening and reception, Reeve was still a little dizzy from the loss of blood, but he managed to make it through the evening. In fact, he eloquently told the audience about his desire to work after the accident. "It was very bleak for me," he said. "I didn't know what I was going to do next. Thanks to the wonderful material that came to me, I feel like I have started a new chapter in my life." He has said, "I'm grateful that in my condition I have a creative outlet." So were his colleagues. *In the Gloaming* was nominated for five Emmys and won four Cable Ace awards, more than any other production that year.

In the meantime, Reeve continued to attend fund-raisers and lobby for health care reform and increased funding for research. On January, 12, 1997, he hosted a fund-raiser in his hometown of Princeton, New Jersey, attended by 1,180 people who paid $75 to $500 to attend. The evening included appearances by several celebrities. "I think God sent Chris to be the man to do this because of his heart and courage and awareness and fight," actor Mandy Patinkin commented that evening. "He's more than Superman."

Entertainers Mary Tyler Moore (at microphones) and Christopher Reeve are joined by members of Congress during a 1998 news conference calling for the doubling of the National Institutes of Health budget. From left to right are Senator Barbara Mikulski, Senator Edward Kennedy, Moore, Senator Paul Wellstone, and Reeve.

Chapter **TWELVE**

DREAMING

EVEN THOUGH HE'S IN A WHEELCHAIR, CHRISTOPHER Reeve is determined to remain active, focusing his efforts in three areas—work, family, and spinal cord injury research. He continues to pursue exciting acting projects. "I'd like to play a character that would show the resourcefulness of a disabled person and also show new technology," he has said.

Since the accident, Reeve has been offered roles of disabled characters many times, but for the most part he hasn't been happy with them. "Often roles about disabled people show them in a pathetic light," he explained. "We need more scripts showing people in a realistic light."

The actor is also a public lecturer and author. Each

Reeve, with his wife, Dana, and his son Will, is honored with a star on the Hollywood Walk of Fame.

year he speaks 30 or 40 times in rehabilitation centers and earns more than $50,000 for speeches to other groups. In addition, Random House paid him $3 million to write his autobiography, *Still Me,* which was published in May 1998.

Reeve continues to campaign for funding so researchers can find a cure for patients with nerve damage. In May 1996, he became chairman of the American Paralysis Association, which works in conjunction with the Christopher Reeve Foundation to raise funds for research.

Although Reeve understands the importance of the work he does outside his home, he cherishes time with his family above all other activities. "[W]hat I found is being with your children is what really counts," he says. Before the accident, he and Will

Dana and Christopher Reeve attend a gathering at which they donated $500,000 from the Christopher Reeve Foundation to the American Paralysis Association.

sailed, threw rocks into the water, or looked for owls in the woods. Now they're happy just to sit together. For four months of the year, Alexandra and Matthew also live with their father.

Reeve dreams about the days when he was mobile. Sometimes he's competing in an equestrian competition or sailing. He calls these nighttime journeys "wonderful adventures" but admits that "[i]t's always a shock when I wake up and realize that I'm a little stuck."

If his real dreams come true, Reeve won't be stuck anymore. And with his help, neither will other spinal cord injury patients.

SOURCES

9   Adrian Havill, *Man of Steel* (USA: Penguin Group, 1996) 6.
9   Ibid., 7.
9   Christopher Reeve, interview, *Larry King Live*, CNN, Los Angeles, 16 April 1997.
9   Havill 13.
9   Roger Rosenblatt, "New Hopes, New Dreams," *Time*, 26 August 1996, 44.
9   Reeve, interview, *Larry King Live*.
9   Rosenblatt 45.
11 Liz Smith, "We Draw Strength from Each Other," *Good Housekeeping*, June 1996, 37.
15 Kathy Larkin, "Christopher Reeve: He's Flying High Without the Cape," *Daily News*, 6 October 1985, 5.
15 Havill, 40.
15 Peter Travers, "Chris Reeve Is 'Superman' And Super Dad—'Ear, 'Ear," *People*, 6 July 1981, 84.
16 Karen S. Schneider, "Local Hero," *People*, 27 January 1997, 84.
17 Roderick Gilchrist, "Superman: He's Cut-glass Good-looking, He's Built Like a Tank But He Plays Ravel," *New York Post*, 4 November 1978, 15.
19 *Christopher Reeve*, interview, *Inside the Actors Studio: The Craft of Theater and Film*, Bravo, 26 February 1997.
20 Kristin McMurran, "It's Stardom, Not Flying, That Christopher Reeve Fears: The Last Superman Shot Himself," *People*, 1 August 1979, 61.
21 Reeve interview, Bravo.
22 "Chris Reeve, Whose Acting Career Began at PDS, Wins Title Role in Forthcoming Film, 'Superman,'" *Princeton Town Topics*, 24 February 1977.
23 Havill, 42.
23 Ibid., 44.
23 Ibid.
24 Blaine Harden, "It's a Bird! it's a Plane! It's Christopher Reeve!" *Trenton Times*, 24 February 1977.
27 Reeve interview, Bravo.

27 "Christopher Reeve to Visit Campus," *Cornell Chronicle*, 11 November 1993. Cybernex ISP. (gopher://gopher.cornell.edu:70/ORO-2238-/.files/CH111193/CH11119327).

28 Warner Brothers Press Department, "Christopher Reeve," undated: 3.

29–30 Ibid.,4.

30 Reeve interview, Bravo.

31 Ibid.

32 Warner Brothers, 5.

32 Larkin, 5.

33 Reeve interview, Bravo.

33 Ibid.

34 Ibid.

34 Robert Wahl, "Krypton's Brightest Star," *Daily News*, 2 November 1980, 4.

34 Havill, 56.

35 Travers, 84.

35 Reeve interview, Bravo.

35 McMurran, 61.

38 Reeve interview, Bravo.

39 Warner Brothers, 1.

39 Gene Siskel, "A Leader by Inspiration," *Chicago Tribune Magazine*, 19 November 1978, 22.

40 Warner Brothers, 1-2.

41 Jerry Roberts, "Peers Pile Praise on Reeve," *Variety*, 29 September 1997, 64.

41 Siskel, 22.

42 *Town Topics*.

43 McMurran, 59.

47–48 "Here Comes Superman!!!" *Time*, 27 November 1978, 61.

48 Reeve interview, Bravo.

49 "Here Comes Superman!!!" 61.

49–50 Christopher Reeve, "Christopher Reeve: Super Chat with Sharon Hammond," *Interview*, December 1978, 52.

50 Warner Brothers, 7.

50 Colin Dangaard, "Actor Leaps Into a Super Role," *New York Post*, 30 July 1977, 42.

51 Reeve interview, Bravo.

52 Reeve interview, Hammond 52.

53 Siskel 22; Gilchrist 15.

53 Nancy Collins, "Super Mania," *Washington Post,*
       11 December 1978.
55 Vincent Canby, "Screen: It's a Bird, It's a Plane, It's a
       Movie," *New York Times,* 15 December 1978.
56 Reeve interview, Hammond 52.
56 Christopher Reeve, interview, with Ruth Matheson,
       INSITE newsletter, May 1979 interview, April 1993 pub.
57 Rex Reed, "Chris Reeve: Look Ma, No Cape," *Daily
       News,* 16 November 1980.
57 Reeve interview, Matheson.
57 Jo Addie, "A Long-Awaited Reunion with Christopher
       Reeve," *Somewhere in Time* Homepage, Cybernex ISP
       (http://homepage.interaccess.com/~addie/facts.html).
59 Reeve interview, Bravo.
61 Ed Naha, "Superman II," *Future Life,* August 1981, 30.
62 Ibid., 31.
62 Ibid.
62 Travers, 82.
63 Ibid., 84.
63 Havill, 8.
63 Jack Martin, "Martin's Sideliners," *New York Post,*
       13 March 1980.
64 Havill, 8.
64 Reed, 14.
64 Carol Lawson, "From Superman to Vietnam Veteran for
       Christopher Reeve," *New York Times,* 5 September
       1980.
65 Vincent Canby, "Screen: 'Somewhere in Time,' a
       Romance," *New York Times,* 3 October 1980.
65 Kathleen Carroll, "This 'Time' A Waster," *Daily News,*
       3 October 1980.
65 Addie, "A Long-Awaited Reunion with Christopher
       Reeve."
66 Reed, 3.
66 Ibid.
66 Ibid., 14
66 Janet Maslin, "Screen: 'Superman II' Is Full of Tricks,"
       New York Times, 19 June 1981.
67 Reed, 3.
67 Reeve interview, Bravo.
69 Sue Russell, "Superman in Love," *USA Today,* 4 August
       1981, 21.

69–70   Ibid.

  70   Ibid.

  71   Roberts, 64.

  71   Sibley, 22.

  72   Roberts, 64.

  72   Diana Maychick, "Out-of-this-world 'Superman' Becomes Worldly 'Monsignor,'" *New York Post*, 19 October 1982.

  73   Peter Donald, "The Man of Steel Exits Nearly Stainless," *TV-Cable Week*, 12 June 1983, 20.

  75   Phil Roura and Tom Poster, "Chris Tosses in Cape as Superman," *Daily News*, 21 June 1983, 9.

  75   Annette Insdorf, "Superman Comes Down to Earth," *New York Daily News*, 29 July 1984, 3.

75–76   Reeve interview, *Larry King Live*.

  77   Sibley, 22.

  77   Ibid., 21.

  79   Julie Salamon, "On Film: Bringing Up (Someone Else's) Baby," *Wall Street Journal*, 26 March 1987, 34.

79–80   Jeannie Park, "Eat Your Heat Out, Lois," *People*, 20 April 1992, 142.

  82   Siskel, 22.

  82   Havill, 176.

  84   Stephen Schaefer, "'Remains' a Reunion for Reeve," *USA Today*, 9 November 1993.

  84   Cindy Adams, "Weasels, Chickens, Turkeys; A Bit of Bond-age for Mel?" *New York Post*, 11 November 1993, 10.

  84   Todd McCarthy, "The Remains of the Day," *Variety*, 4 October 1993, 38.

  85   Kendall Hamilton, "A Tragic Fall for Superman," *Newsweek*, 12 June 1995, 43.

  85   Havill, 19.

  88   Smith, 88.

  88   Ibid.

  89   "Statement from the Reeve Family," Charlottesville, Virginia, 31 May 1995.

  90   Linda Massarella, "Reeve Greets Doctor with a Smile After 6-hour Surgery," *New York Post*, June 6, 1995, 14.

  91   John Jane, press briefing, University of Virginia Medical Center, Charlottesville, Virginia, 5 June 1995.

91   Dana Reeve, statement, UVa Medical Center,
      Charlottesville, Virginia, 9 June 1995.
92   Dana Reeve, statement, 9 June 1995.
92   Schneider, 86.
93   "The Will to Live," *People*, 26 June 1995, 56.
93   Smith, 88.
93   Rosenblatt, 46.
96   Ibid.
96–97 Christopher Reeve, interview, *Today*, with Katie Couric,
      NBC, New York, N.Y., 28 November 1995.
97   Ibid.
99   Rosenblatt, 50.
104   Claudia Puig, "A Challenge That Reeve Couldn't
      Refuse," *Los Angeles Times*, 28 March 1996.
105   Annie Groer and Ann Gerhart, "Reeve, Playing to a
      Packed House," *Washington Post*, 16 May 1996.
106   Rosenblatt, 50.
109   Christopher Reeve, speech at DNC Convention, United
      Center, Chicago, Illinois, 26 August 1996.
110   Diane Goldner, "Reeve's Selflessness Part of
      Rehabilitation," *Variety*, 29 September 1997, New York
      supplement, 64.
110   Michael Kilian, "Wresting Good from Tragedy,
      Christopher Reeve Moves in a New Direction,"
      Chicago Tribune, 28 March 1997, Tempo sec., 1.
110–111 Diane Goldner, "Role Behind Camera Comes to the
      Fore," *Variety*, 9 September 1997, New York
      supplement, 60.
112   Lawrie Mifflin, "After a Life in Front of a Camera, a
      New One Behind It," *New York Times*, 31 October
      1996, C15.
112   Mifflin, C15.
113   Goldner, "Role Behind Camera Comes to the Fore," 59.
115   Reeve, interview, Bravo.
115   Schneider, 84.
115   Reeve interview, *Larry King Live*.
117   Goldner, "Role Behind Camera Comes to the Fore," 60.
117   Reeve interview, *Larry King Live*.
118   Smith, 88.
119   *Christopher Reeve: A Celebration of Hope*, prod. Don
      Mischer, ABC, Los Angeles, 1 March 1998.

BIBLIOGRAPHY

Adams, Cindy. "Weasels, Chickens, Turkey; a Bit of Bond-age for Mel?" *New York Post*, 11 November 1993, 10.

Addie, Jo. "A Long-Awaited Reunion with Christopher Reeve." *Somewhere in Time Home Page.* n.d., <http://homepage.interaccess.com/~addie/reunion.html>.

Canby, Vincent. "It's a Bird, It's a Plane, It's a Movie." *New York Times*, 15 December 1978, sec. C, p. 15.

Carrol, Kathleen. "This 'Time' a Waster." *New York Daily News*, 3 October 1980, 21.

"Chris Reeve, Whose Acting Career Began at PDS, Wins Title Role in Forthcoming Film, 'Superman.'" *Princeton Town Topics* [New Jersey], 24 February 1977, sec. B.

Christopher Reeve: A Celebration of Hope. Producer Don Mischer. Los Angeles, ABC, 1 March 1998.

"Christopher Reeve to Visit Cornell Campus." *Cornell Chronicle*, 11 November 1993, <gopher://gopher.cornell.edu:70/ORO-4282-/.files/CH111193/CH11119327>.

Collins, Nancy. "Super Mania." *Washington Post*, 11 December 1978, sec. B, 1.

Dangaard, Colin. "Actor Leaps into a Super Role." *New York Post*, 30 July 1977, 42.

Donald, Peter. "The Man of Steel Exits Nearly Stainless." *TV-Cable Week*, 12 June 1983, 20–23.

Gilchrist, Roderick. "Superman: Cut-Glass Good-Looking, He's Built Like a Tank but He Plays Ravel." *New York Post*, 4 November 1978, 15.

Goldner, Diane. "Reeve's Selflessness Part of Rehabilitation." *Variety*, 29 September 1997, New York supplement, 60.

Goldner, Diane. "Role Behind Camera Comes to the Fore." *Variety*, 29 September 1997, New York supplement, 59–60.

Goldsborough, Robert. Letter. *Chicago Tribune Magazine*, 19 November 1978, 7.

Groer, Annie and Ann Gerhart. "Reeve, Playing to a Packed House." *Washington Post*, 16 May 1996, sec. C, p. 3.

Hamilton, Kendall. "A Tragic Fall for Superman." *Newsweek*, 12 June 1995, 43.

Harden, Blaine. "It's a Bird! It's a Plane! It's Christopher Reeve!" *Trenton Times*, 24 February 1977, sec. A, p. 1.

Havill, Adrian. *Man of Steel*. USA: Penguin Group, 1996.

"Here Comes Superman!!!" *Time*, 27 November 1978, 59–61.

Insdorf, Annette. "Superman Comes Down to Earth." *New York Daily News*, 29 July 1984, 3.

Jane, John. Press briefing. UVa Medical Center. Charlottesville, Virginia, 2 June 1995.

Kilian, Michael. "Wresting Good from Tragedy, Christopher Reeve Moves in a New Direction." *Chicago Tribune*, north sports final ed., Tempo sec., p. 1.

Larkin, Kathy. "Christopher Reeve: He's Flying High Without the Cape." *New York Daily News*, 6 October 1985, 4–5.

Lawson, Carol. "From Superman to Vietnam Veteran for Christopher Reeve." *New York Times*, 5 September 1980, sec. C, p. 2.

McCarthy, Todd. "The Remains of the Day." *Variety*, 4 October 1993, 38.

McMurran, Kristin. "It's Stardom, Not Flying, That Christopher Reeve Fears: The Last Superman Shot Himself." *People*, 8 January 1979, 58–60.

Martin, Jack. "Martin's Sideliners." *New York Post*, 13 March 1980, 7.

Maslin, Janet. "Screen: 'Superman II' is Full of Tricks." *New York Times*, 19 June 1981, sec. C, p. 8.

Massarella, Linda. "Reeve Greets Doctor with a Smile after 6-Hour Surgery." *New York Post*, 6 June 1995, 14.

Maychick, Diana. "Out-of-This-World 'Superman' Becomes Worldly Monsignor." *New York Post*, 19 October 1982, 34.

Mifflin, Lawrie. "After a Life in Front of a Camera, a New One behind It." *New York Times*, 31 October 1996, sec C, p. 15.

Naha, Ed. "Superman II." *Future Life*, August 1981, 28–32.

Park, Jeannie. "Eat Your Heart Out, Lois." *People*, 20 April 1992, 141–143.

Puig, Claudia. "A Challenge That Reeve Couldn't Refuse." *Los Angeles Times*, 28 March 1996, sec. F, p. 1.

Reed, Rex. "Chris Reeve: Look Ma, No Cape." *New York Daily News*, 16 November 1980, 3.

Reeve, Christopher. "Christopher Reeve: Super Chat with Sharon
    Hammond." *Interview,* December 1978, 52–53.
———. "Inside the Actors Studio: The Craft of Theater and
    Film." With James Lipton. Bravo. 26 February 1997.
———. Interview by Katie Couric, *Today.* NBC, 28 November 1995.
———. Interview by Ruth Matheson. In INSITE newsletter, April
    1993.
———. Interview by Larry King, *Larry King Live.* CNN, 16 April
    1997.
———. Speech read at DNC Convention, Chicago, August 1996.
Reeve, Dana. Statement. UVa Medical Center. Charlottesville, VA,
    9 June 1995.
Rosenblatt, Roger. "New Hopes, New Dreams." *Time,* 26 August
    1996, 40–52.
Roura, Phil, and Tom Poster. "Chris Tosses in Cape As
    Superman." *New York Daily News,* 21 June 1983, 9.
Salamon, Julie. "On Film" Bringing up (Someone Else's) Baby."
    Wall Street Journal, 26 March 1987, p. 34.
Schaefer, Stephen. "'Remains' a Reunion for Reeve." *USA Today,*
    9 November 1993, sec. D, p. 2.
Schneider, Karen S. "Local Hero." *People Weekly,* 27 January
    1997, 82–86.
Sibley, Adrian. "Superman and Beyond." *Films and Filming,*
    March 1987, 20–23.
Siskel, Gene. "A Leader by Inspiration." *Chicago Tribune*
    Magazine, 19 November 1978, 22.
Smith, Liz. "We Draw Strength from Each Other." *Good
    Housekeeping,* June 1996, 86.
Travers, Peter. "Chris Reeve is 'Superman' and Super Dad—'Ear,
    'Ear." *People,* 6 July 1981, 82–86.
Wahl, Robert. "Krypton's Brightest Star." *New York Daily News,*
    2 November 1980, 4.
Warner Brothers Press Department. "Christopher Reeve." n.d. 1–7.
"The Will to Live." *People,* 26 June 1995, 55–56.
Wilson, Earl. "Superman Super." *New York Post,* 16 November
    1978, 50.

INDEX

ABOUT THE AUTHOR

Megan Howard has written eleven books for children and teenagers. Her work has also appeared in *Seventeen* and *Entertainment Weekly* magazines. When she's not writing, Megan enjoys gardening, reading, and cooking. She lives in New Jersey with her husband and son.

AUTHOR ACKNOWLEDGMENTS

Thanks to Deb Fehr at Williamstown Theater, Beth Hamilton and Marcy Decker at Cornell University, Laura Lee Juliano at Old Globe Theatre, Marguerite Beck at UVa Medical Center, Carl Fretts and Arnold Jones Jr. for their research assistance. Special thanks to Kathy Duke, who shared her knowledge of equestrian jumping.

Of course, I'm also deeply grateful to Bruce and Jed for all their support and advice. They are my super men.

PHOTO ACKNOWLEDGMENTS

Agence France Presse/Corbis-Bettmann, 99; © David Allen/Corbis, 109; AP/Wide World Photos, 6, 8, 14, 96, 100, 111, 112, 114, 117; Archive Photos, 26, 66; Popperfoto/Archive Photos, 26; Frank Edwards/Fotos International/Archive Photos, 32; Express Newspapers/Archive Photos, 60; Cannon (courtesy Kobal), 77; Superman is a trademark of DC Comics, © 1998. All rights reserved. 40; © Steve Finn/Alpha/Globe Photos, Inc., 95 (both); Globe Photos, Inc., 58, 64, 71, 80, © Bob Deutsch/Globe Photos, Inc., 46, © Judie Burstein, Globe Photos, Inc. 53; © David Parker/Globe Photos, Inc., 75; © Michael Ferguson/Globe Photos, Inc., 83; © James M. Kelly/Globe Photos, Inc., 89, 90, 98; © Fitzroy Barrett/Globe Photos, Inc., 116 (both); Hollywood Book & Poster, 76; © Kevin Mazur/London Features International (USA) Ltd., 86; Suzanne Murphy-Larronde, 93; Billy Rose Theatre Collection, The New York Public Library for the Performing Arts, Astor, Lenox, and Tilden Foundations, 33; Old Globe Theatre, 28; Photofest, 2, 36, 38, 44, 47, 50, 51, 54, 72, 73; Seth Poppel Yearbook Archives, 12,18, 23, 24; Princeton University Libraries, 20, 22; Reuters/Gary Hershorn/Archive Photos, 106; UPI/Corbis-Bettmann, 74; Warner Brothers (courtesy Kobal), 41, 70; Williamstown Theatre Festival Archives, 21, 67, 68; Wisconsin Center for Film and Theater Research, 30; © Vinnie Zuffante/Star File, Inc., 82.

Front cover, © Andrea Renault/Globe Photos, Inc.; back cover, Globe Photos, Inc.